Dedication

There are many people that I would like to dedicate this book to. People like my Mom who never stopped my growth and only inspired me to keep going, my best friends who never left my side no matter what happened, and most of all, to Prescilla, for showing me that poetry doesn't always have to be sad. Thank you for showing me the joys of being in love.

I love you

Hidden Chaos

They question our madness

And call it words like "sublime"

But this amount of sadness

Is definitely not divine

You see this chaos inside me

I wish it were gone

For it forces me to see

Everything I've done wrong

And I cannot fall asleep

Because I am threatened to stay

In my position with no meep

While keeping my demons at bay

I am afraid to feel love

With all of its beauty and charm

For it is too up above

And bringing it down will cause harm

Yet you still see me move

And act through a day

Well its only to soothe

A small part of the pain

So please do not fear me

For I already fear myself

Instead just smile with glee

And put me to rest on your shelf

Brightest Sun

I tell you I am fine

And nothings on my mind

For this pain that is mine

Can only heal with time

But the days I am weak

You will find what you seek

I might be at my peak

And fall down in defeat

For once I had a sun

It was the brightest one

She put air in my lungs

But that sun is now done

It burned in its own mark

And left my body dark

So I put it in park

And reversed to the start

I cannot fill this hole

Left vacant of a soul

For the sun that you stole

Has left me craving control

Until That Day

There will come a day

When I push you away

But what I really want

Is for you to stay

It has come to the point

Where love and fear come in joint

And the reason I stopped

Is to not disappoint

I don't cry out of pity

Until sleep finally hits me

Because I have learned

That is not the key

I wait for the day

When someone comes to say

"I will make you happy,

Everything will be ok"

So until that day comes

I will follow the crumbs

That hopefully lead me

To something good to become

Take Them All

Take all of my memories

Take my whole share

Remember the happiness

And become aware

You meant more than just words

Or figures of speech

You guided me towards

Places I could not reach

So even if it takes

My memories being taken

I hope for God's sake

That you will finally awaken

He Better Be Better

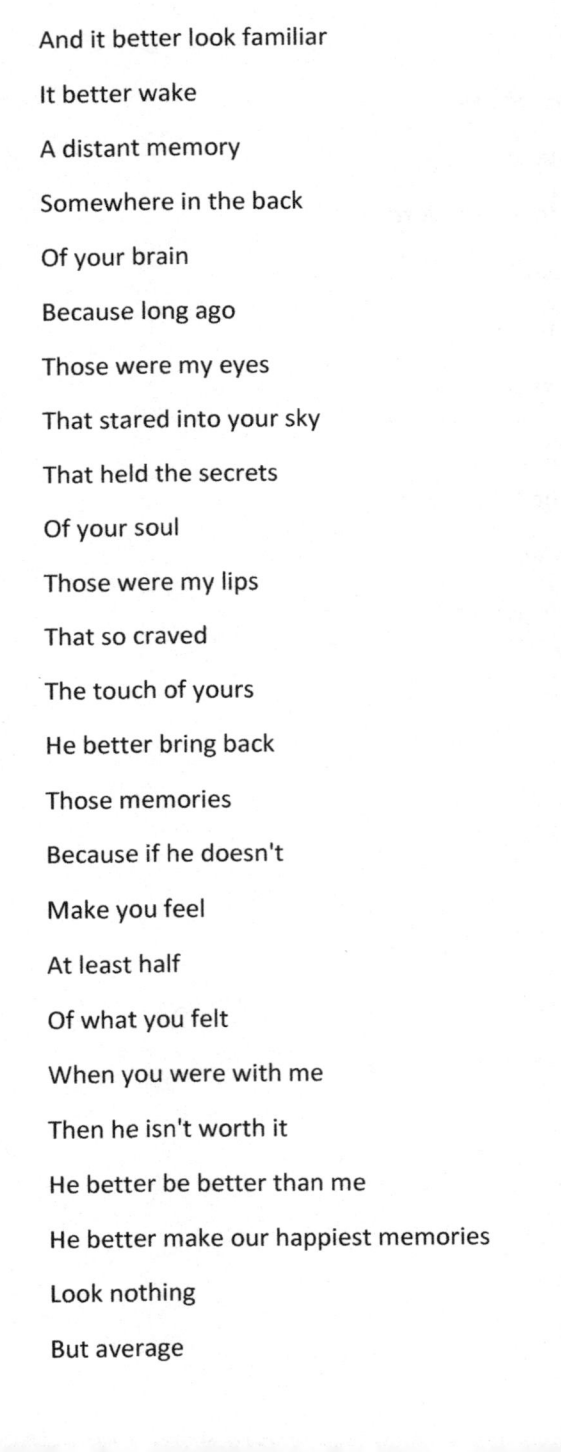

I can just imagine

The way he

Looks at you

And it better look familiar

It better wake

A distant memory

Somewhere in the back

Of your brain

Because long ago

Those were my eyes

That stared into your sky

That held the secrets

Of your soul

Those were my lips

That so craved

The touch of yours

He better bring back

Those memories

Because if he doesn't

Make you feel

At least half

Of what you felt

When you were with me

Then he isn't worth it

He better be better than me

He better make our happiest memories

Look nothing

But average

In My Dreams

I sit up on my bed

After a cold night of slumber

With tears coming from my eyes

"I must have had a nightmare"

I thought

So I sit to remember what it was

And the more I thought

The more I saw

You and I

Both still happy

Both still together

As one

Both living life perfectly

I felt so happy

I asked you to stay

Here

And you said you would

"But only in your dreams"

You kissed me and sent me off

I sit up on my bed

With tears coming from my eyes

"I must have had a nightmare"

I thought

Indeed it was

But one I would

Like to have

Again and again

Because if you settle

For anyone less

Well

That would be

The greatest revenge

Against yourself

Reality

There are times

When I find myself

Thinking of you

It is not all the time

But only on rare occasions

And on even

Rarer occasions

I wonder if you were

Ever real

Sometimes I forget

What your lips tasted like

How soft your skin was

What color your hair would shine in the sun

How radiant your smile was

What your laugh sounded like

What your favorite food was

I forget so much more

To the point where I question

Your entire existence in my life

But that quickly leaves

Because the one thing

I cannot forget

Was how you made me feel

That is my proof of you

The happiness that you gave me

That you lent me

Does not leave my mind

It is destined

To stay with me

Forever

I wish that were the case

For all of you

Do They Know?

I hear them talk

And I ask myself

Do they know?

They mention you as if

You were nothing

Do you mention me like that?

They say your name

As smooth as a running river

And I shatter every time

Do they know

How much it hurts

To remember you?

To remember us?

I'm sure they don't

Because those who do

Do not even mention you

I hope they find out

Or you tell them

So they won't keep

Causing avalanches

In my heart

Because of you

I don't know my worth

Actually, that is not true

I know what I am not worth

Because of you

My love remains lost

Inside the desolate wasteland

That is your heart

And I cannot get it back

Because of you

When I finally hear these words

I automatically assume it's false

And I cast them aside

Because of you

But because of you

I know who to avoid

What not to do

How not to act

And how to give space

Because of you

I do not worry about

The littlest things

Nor do I run away

From the biggest threat

Because of you

I know the difference between

You and her

And quite frankly my dear

If it weren't for you

I would have never found her

Thank you

Something On My Mind

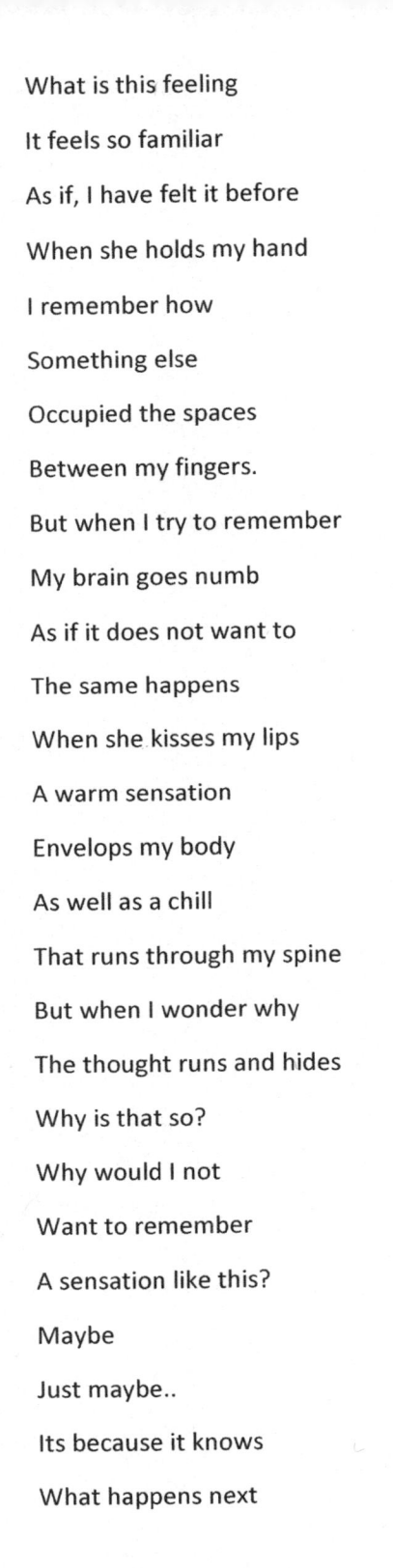

What is this feeling

It feels so familiar

As if, I have felt it before

When she holds my hand

I remember how

Something else

Occupied the spaces

Between my fingers.

But when I try to remember

My brain goes numb

As if it does not want to

The same happens

When she kisses my lips

A warm sensation

Envelops my body

As well as a chill

That runs through my spine

But when I wonder why

The thought runs and hides

Why is that so?

Why would I not

Want to remember

A sensation like this?

Maybe

Just maybe..

Its because it knows

What happens next

Darkness

The more you live in the darkness

The harder it is to leave

But you eventually do

And when you step into the light

The light that you have forever longed for

You do not know what to do

You spent so much time wandering

That now that you are not lost

You have lost your purpose of being found

Maybe you left it in the darkness

So you go back and look

Like a blind man searching

For something he cannot touch

And you get lost again

And the whole cycle repeats

Those who are lost in the darkness

Crave being found

But once they are

They succumb to it much easier

The darkness was always there for us

Even when we didn't want it

Especially when we didn't want it

But it is the only thing we know

A Change in The Winds

My eyes have been opened

To the image of something grand

Because now instead of hoping

Things are going according to plan

The idea of becoming right

Is no longer impossible

The future is bright

And now seems plausible

My heart was once broken

By who I dubbed as the villain

But it was words left unspoken

That drove the last nail in

I have come to peace with my flaws

And her methods of ending it

And it feels like her claws

Are no longer choking my neck

And to cap it all off

A girl comes to me

She says she's had enough

Because of me she can see

She showers me with love

Until I am drowning

And when I stick my head above

I never see her frowning

I am almost afraid

Of this happy moment in time

So I start looking for aid

Before I see the signs

I know it is foolish

To look for the end

I know too how useless

It is to crack at every bend

So I will enjoy my time with her

Until fate sees fit

May it be til November

Or even longer than I'm scared to admit

Dog on a Leash

I am a dog on a leash

Who cannot find peace

Because of the piece

You refuse to release

My leash knows no bounds

There is no way around

Whether I skip across town

Or just dig straight down

Sometimes it disappears

And I stay in fear

For it might again appear

And drag me back to here

I do not want to stay

Like this every day

I wonder if it may

Actually ever go away

The Tortured Mind

You refuse to leave me be

Oh why can you not see

That this emotion is called happy

And it is without thee

You broke my heart in two

Then shattered it into

Small pieces for you

To rebuild and redo

And you keep this cycle going

Very damn well knowing

That these wounds that you keep sewing

Only keep puncturing

I give you my heart

But you refuse to take part

Then shoot back like a dart

And refuse to be apart

Then tell me what you want

Is your motive just to taunt

Or is it hidden within the font

That leaves me crying like an enfant

It is these thoughts that make me worried

About myself and make me scurry

To a happy place with hurry

And leave those thoughts buried.

How Ironic, Don't You Think?

I remember how you treated me

How you made me feel like I was nothing

You made me want to apologize for my very existence

And the pain that I so charmingly caused you

But who was the one to blame

The fool who ran after his heart

Or the girl who left breadcrumbs to be followed

Who is the one who hurt the most

The man who turned a blind eye to all the bad

And let it eat away until he was nothing but

Blood and bones

Or the woman who knew it would never work

But tried and tried because she couldn't bear

To see him cry

Who is the one who should move on first

The guy who gave his heart to one girl and is still waiting to receive it all back

Or the lady who could not give her heart when she herself has no idea how it works

The reality is that I have found a new love

I cannot give her my everything because I am not complete

But I give her the rest of what I have

Because she gives me the same

And I know it can happen to you

I know it can happen to you

For you are stronger than I am

And although strength alone does not guarantee success

It is definitely useful in fighting through

The fog and confusion

Check My Resume

I made you a promise

To not be one of those memories

That would haunt you with the start

Of every new conversation

But I have much experience in the art

Of breaking promises

I should show you my resume

But just because it happened

Does not mean it is right

I miss the feeling of us laughing

Or even us crying

Or even us trying

To get through life without dying

Because life was deemed worthy to live

When you my time I would give

And I know it does not matter

You have found your way out of misery

Or at least that's what it looks like

But I know how much it hurts to fake

Being ok

Almost as much as turning out the light in your room

And the light outside doesn't shine through your window

And that darkness that you so ever fear

Inches closer and closer all around you

At least your irrational fears are all made up

Your physical pain that you feel in your heart

Is similar to mine

I rushed into thinking that I was going to lose you

And ended up pushing you away instead

Another note to add to my resume

Flames Still Burn

This idea of separation

Comes with the invasion

Of dark thoughts into my thinking station

That stay no matter how many times

My brain goes into a state of revision

I never feared being forgotten

Until I experienced forgetting everything

And realized how many memories can be lost

When you act without thinking of the cost

Or go up to a situation with accost

And just toss aside the things that matter most

For I do not start conversations because I do not

Want to be the guy who taught you that people

Are bad and should be avoided at all cost

I was never afraid of talking to someone

Until the day I hurt the one person who didn't

Deserve to

And yes she stole my heart

And ripped it all apart

But it was only because of the fact that

She herself needed to win back the control

That was stolen from her from the villains

Of her past mistakes

Her only mistake was trying to give

What she did not own

She tried to express feelings that she did not

Believe in

She tried to soothe the fire found inside her

With the fire of another flame

But only ended up stealing each others' oxygen

What she does not know is that both flames still

Burn with love and passion

But with experience comes the consequence

Of knowing that pain must be felt in order to

Fully enjoy the happiness that is awarded to us

I was never afraid of showing others my flame

But now I know what it is like to get burned

Which has in turn

Caused me to yearn

For the solitary and churn

At the sight of happiness

Because I do believe in happy endings

Just not for people like me

The Small Things

It has been almost a year since I last saw you

But the thing with technology is that

I cannot avoid seeing you

Especially when you hang out with our friends

It was bound to happen eventually

And yet, when it did, I was taken

Completely by surprise

Seeing you was something I wanted to avoid

Because I didn't know how I would react

I don't know if I would hate you

I don't know if I would love you

I don't know if I'd be able to take it

But as I stared at that video of you

The only thought that came to my head:

"Your hair isn't short anymore"

25 Minutes Away

The hardest part about

Getting over you

Was forgetting all of

Our best and happiest moments

Like the last one we ever shared

When you invited me to the place

Where you live

And realized it was only

A 25 minute walk away

Oh how many of our problems

Could have been solved

Had I known that from the start

I could have reached your home

In less than an hour

And talked it out with you

And now every time I drive by

I remember this fact

And the process starts again

Broken Engine

The thing about broken hearts

Is that they can never be fixed

Using the same pieces

You wouldn't use the same broken engine after an accident

Instead, you replace the broken bits

With similar but different pieces

Only by giving up on the broken pieces

Can one move on and restore

Something beautiful

Beating Hearts

I made the decision

To give my heart away

And in the end

I didn't get all of it back

I searched and searched for the missing parts

Until I finally gave up

"I can live life without a complete heart"

What a ridiculous thought

All of the time spent before you

Was just me living a lie

Pretending to be ok

Pretending to live

Pretending to beat

But then you came along

You were also missing pieces of your heart

And how convenient

Your missing parts

Matched my complete parts perfectly

Now, her and I share the same heart

It does not beat the same as before

For we were born with different tunes

But slowly, I feel it coming together

Synchronizing

I anxiously wait for the day

When our heart beats as one

That will be the day

That you will see just how much

I can love you

That's the thing about pain...

Have you ever wondered why

Pain

Can be so relatable?

Most of my writings are about pain

Because I feel like most can relate

After all, we have all experienced pain before

And reading about it makes us feel connected

After thinking, I find that idea frightening

And discouraging

But imagine,

Just imagine for a bit

If everyone in the world

Could relate to a piece of writing

Associated with love?

If someone can look at a loving couple

And smile because they can feel the love

Wouldn't that be beautiful?

I write about pain because it's the easiest thing

To write about

But now and then, I challenge myself

To write about how love makes me feel

And hope that all of you

Will know come due time

Exactly how I feel

Prescilla

I look at our pictures

And videos together

I feel such a happiness

I've never been better

For stormy and dark

Were my types of weather

But now I am free

Like a wind-drifting feather

I remember not wanting

This love, this emotion

For it was too little reward

For such a commotion

But you slipped in my drink

Turned it into a potion

And I chugged it all down

And set forth the motion

Now looking back

I have no regrets

Not even the scratches

Not even the dents

For each one added character

I need not repent

For I deserved an angel

And it was you heaven sent

In The Dark

You drive, focused on the night road

Tell me, what would happen if to you I told

That it is your hand I want to hold

Until the days we both grow old?

Tell me, would your response be the same?

Would my heart under you be tamed?

Would the emotion I feel less be pain?

Would my brain finally become sane?

Because I can assure you

That I have these visions too

Visions of only us two

With everything done and not much to do

But in them, our emotions remain intact

Albeit a little compact

But they always come back

From where they retract

So tell me, when you drive in the dark

Do you think of where to park?

Because that should be the easiest part

You belong right here, in my heart

How We Met

Everything I've said

Everything I've done

Is vanished and laid to bed

Because of a certain someone

For I developed a trait

That I thought would stay for life

It was just as strong as hate

And held me dangerously close to the knife

And I did suffer some scars

To both my spirit and my heart

I was locked behind the bars

That would not let me depart

Then suddenly a message

No, more like a symbol

It was a road running through a passage

With what looked like a cymbal

I spent months trying to decipher

This symbol of confusion

Until the day I met her

She looked more like an illusion

She looked like an angel

Falling gracefully down to earth

"Oh why must you taunt me when I am unable

To stand on my legs and prove my worth?"

But the angel suddenly stopped

And glared into my eyes

"For it was I who stared and hoped

For evil to cut their ties"

"But when I saw them not stop

I raced down from heaven up above

My tears forming freezing raindrops

As I hurried to protect the one I love"

The angel's words broke apart my bars

And sent my soul screaming with joy

The lights around me turned into racing cars

For I was no longer a whipping boy

I dove into her arms

All the spirits inside vanquished

They were called away by sounding alarms

And took with them my anguish

"Finally, I am free"

Were the only words I muttered

"Indeed now you can see

That everything else, only left you stuttered."

My Best Mistake

In her I saw everything

I saw my future in a bright light

Walking along with her on a beach

Growing old and talking about the weather

But in her mind

I was never anything more

Than an obstacle in her way

Something like a lost puppy

That she couldn't take home

And no matter where she went

I followed

Hoping that she would one day

If I showed just how much I loved her

She would take me home

But that never happened...

.

.

.

.

And thank God she didn't.

Circle Of Life

Isn't it funny just how things happen?

One day I'm promising my life to someone

And the next, she's throwing me away

But that is just the downside

On the upside,

I can promise to always be waiting for her

And the next thing I know, I'm wondering

How I could ever live without the person

I'm with now

In My Eyes

Look into my eyes

Can you see what I have seen?

What I have felt?

What has been done to me?

What I have done to myself?

You can't?

That's good

Because everything that has happened

Is long gone

All that matters now

Is having you by my side

Only you can hide the pain

In my eyes

After A While

After a while,

You stop believing in yourself.

Instead of hoping to be

Remembered as someone great,

You hope that they learn to

Stay away from people

Like you.

For you know what

You are like.

You realize that

Everything great that has

Ever occurred to you has

Been ruined by none other

Than you.

Why bother for anything else?

Make it your duty to love

Everyone with vast amounts

Of affection.

Break their hearts,

Not in half,

But by filling it and filling it

Until it bursts.

She Was An Angel

She was an Angel

And I tried to

Keep her down

by breaking her

Wings

I didn't know any other way

She came to me when everything I had

Was shattered and thrown into the trash

I was led to believe that it was

My fault

And perhaps it was my fault

For trying my best

Knowing that I might fail

Knowing that once I was out of myself to give

I wouldn't have enough left for me

And yet I tried

And when she came to my rescue

Ignoring the pleas to abandon all hope

For the useless and discarded

She came to me

What was I to do with such happiness?

For what was expected when the time came

For her to ascend back to her home

What could I, a man freshly put back whole

Do to make the blessing remain?

In my mind, it was simple.

Turn the blessing into a curse

I Miss You So Much

I miss you so much

But not enough

To put you through

The chaos going on

Inside my head

Fortunate are the ones

Who have made the

Journey and claim to be untouched

Many have fallen or at the very least

Been swayed by my exploits

Yet believe me, I take no pleasure

In this fact

Walls are built for 2 reasons:

To keep things in

Or

To keep things out

For me, I am the wall

Both trying to push back those

Who wish to enter

And

Hold back the dangers locked inside

Should one finally break through

Then no mercy would be shown

It Doesn't Matter What I Want

It doesn't matter what

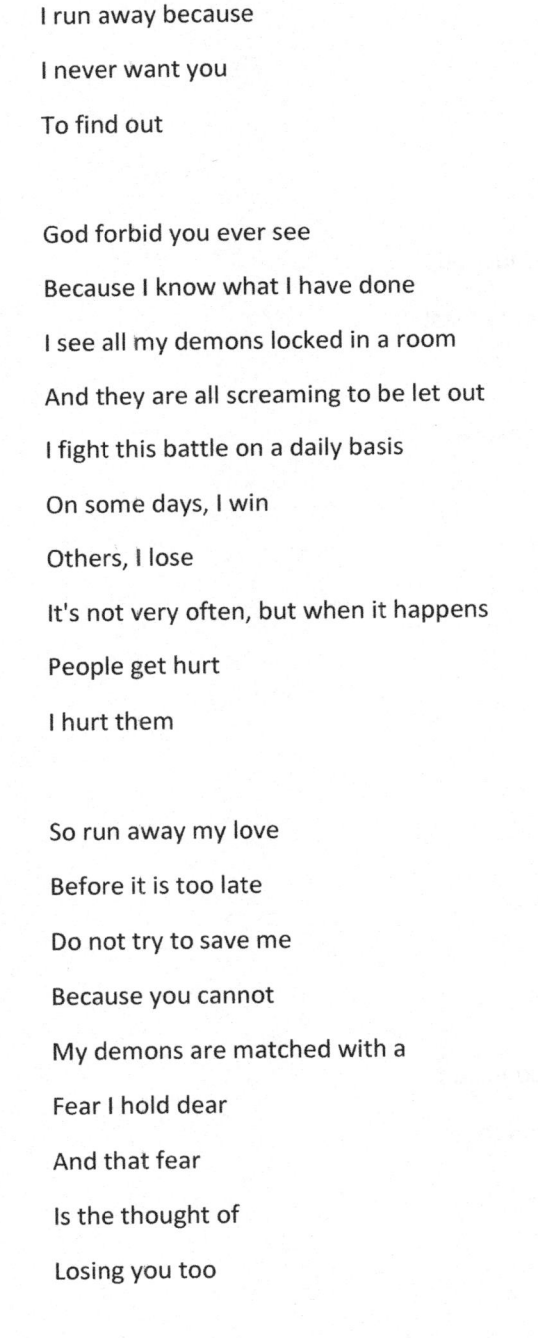

I want

I know what I am

Capable of

I run away because

I never want you

To find out

God forbid you ever see

Because I know what I have done

I see all my demons locked in a room

And they are all screaming to be let out

I fight this battle on a daily basis

On some days, I win

Others, I lose

It's not very often, but when it happens

People get hurt

I hurt them

So run away my love

Before it is too late

Do not try to save me

Because you cannot

My demons are matched with a

Fear I hold dear

And that fear

Is the thought of

Losing you too

I Used To Be Scared Of The Dark

I used to be scared of the dark

I would fear the monsters getting me

And ending my life

But the day I stopped fearing death

Was the day I finally welcomed them

Unfortunately, they never came back

I was so disappointed

I was finally ready

My life has no meaning, I understand now

So why won't they just get it over with

Death is my friend

I welcome it gladly

It was a mistake in my part

To do Death's job

The scars on my wrist display

That failure of mine

But now that I wish

For Death to come swiftly

It is no where to be found

Life is cruel

It wouldn't be right

To make it that easy

Safety Net

I tried to do the things

That made me happy

Everyone of them had lost it's spark

Even the ones I had kept to myself

Were screaming out her name

There was no place for me

To run to

Because I would always

Seek her out

But I broke that safety net

And the knife is still in my hands

So here I am falling

Pretending that I'm flying

Acting like this is all going

According to plan

But the pain in my soul

Refused to let go

I'll eventually land

On the cold concrete floor

I won't pick myself up

Instead I'll just lay as I landed

For the fear of falling as soon

As I start standing

And hope that this floor

Does not sink anymore

Nightmare

Oh I find it ironic

When I am told

To believe in myself

How can I believe

When I do not know

Who I am

One day I fell in love

And then I was hurt

But I was told that I was loved

And for a while I believed it

But that truth eventually faded

Along with every hope I held

Like the chance to get married

Or grow sickly together

I was viciously awoken

From a dream too good to be true

And they expect me to fall asleep again

A dream that turned into reality

Realist almost as cruel

As a nightmare

Please understand

That I don't know when I am dreaming

I am broken

I am broken

Pieces of me are scattered

Across the cosmos

Pieces of love

Pieces of hate

Pieces of trust

Pieces of disappointment

Pieces of memories

That I try to forget

Pieces of emotions that cannot

Be molded into words

But I cannot

Find the motivation

To search

And put myself back together.

Promises

You said you loved me

Was that just a lie?

Was I just someone

You were passing by?

Because when you crossed

From your life in mine

I thought for a bit

That it was my time

You stopped for a chat

And made me believe

I just never thought

How fast you would leave

Along with my heart

You took my happiness

Which I barely found

When you helped me see

I went on a hunt

To find you again

But realized then

I was a bloodstain

The good thing about

Living with no heart

The pain that I feel

Can't be told apart

Get Lost

Ask me how many times I get lost

Looking at you

I wouldn't be able to give you a solid answer

For I started way before

I was actually allowed to

Before you were mine

And I was yours

Before I could ever picture

Spending my life with

The girl with the blonde hair

And beautiful eyes

And I am terrified

That one day

I will get so lost

That I won't be able to find my way back

And by the time I do

You'll be gone

So baby girl

Hold my hand and never let go

This journey that I constantly take

Must not be taken alone

No Regrets

In my life, I have made many mistakes

Many regrets that to this day

Still linger deep in my mind

Actions that I regret taking

Words that I regret speaking

People that I regret meeting

There are days when I wish

To take them all back

And make it right

But the more I think about it

If there is even the slightest

Smallest

Miniscule chance

That everything had to happen

In order to end up with you

Then I would rather not take the risk

And just be happy

Living with you

And all of my regrets

Jealous

I never thought I'd be the jealous type

No one has ever come along to make me jealous

But every time you talk about

The places you'd go

Or the guys you would talk to

Or the things you would do

I can't help but hate it

I hate not knowing you before

For taking so long to find you

I hate everyone who knew you before

Who have seen you grow up

To be honest

I don't hate them

I'm just jealous

That you've been a part of their life's

Longer than mine

Never This Cold

And what am I supposed to do

When the bed beside me is cold

Your warmth is no where to be found

"I'll be back in a few days"

But what am I supposed to do

While I wait for you to come back

I cannot rest without my arms around you

For the bed was never this cold

Until you came along

Maybe I ignored the cold before

But how could I now

When the heat is all I know

So I will sit

And wait

Underneath the covers

Shivering from the cold

Wandering Mind

My mind is often caught

Wandering into where

It does not belong

It imagines people

Places

Events that are better left

Unsaid

And as chaotic as it sounds

There are small occasions

When I'm glad I did

For example

When I began remembering

My past relationship

And I would constantly

Confuse her

With you

Because although I thought of her

You never leave my mind

Peace Of Mind

The mistakes we make

Are ours alone

But that does not mean

That only we suffer the consequences

There are plenty of times

When I have made the wrong choice

And the people I love

Are affected worse

If I could, I would redo all of them

But my dense mind would most likely

Follow the same road

Imagine if our minds were 100%

Under our own control

Speaking of that, how funny that

We cannot control it completely

Millions of years of evolution

And the same underlying problem

Is the inability to understand

Our incoherent thoughts

If I could control my mind

I would tell it to finally

Let you go

To finally move on in life

To make an effort at a happy ending

Light

My mother asks why I

Do not write many positive pieces

"Writing about the dark

Will not make it any easier to

see the light" She might be right

But at the same time, she is not

I will not say that I hate the light

Or contraire,

I am in love with it

It is the one thing that makes

Life worth living

But it is frightening

Once you see the light

You spend the rest of your life

Chasing it

And that is no metaphor

It becomes the one thing

You cannot live without

Through pain and misery

You follow it

Just hoping

To feel it on your skin

Once more

But my skin is burned

My eyes are blinded from the light

Ears blown from my own screams

I do not remember the light

Her

For some women

Their dream is to find

That special someone who will

Love them and make them happy

Forever

That is also my dream

To find the woman who

Deserves my love and who

Would gladly take my last name

Always

Most people spend

Years searching for that

One person to make that dream

Come true

How lucky am I

To have already found

Her

Every Detail

Believe me, I agree that the overthinking

Is bad and should be controlled

But I like to look at Silver linings

And one of them is my attention to detail

And whether you believe me or not

I'm always paying attention to detail

Whether it's when we're walking

And I shorten my stride to match yours

Or I put my hand over the middle console

Because it's hot and I don't want you to

Burn yourself

Or if we're standing outside

And I put myself between you and the sun

To cast some shade down on you

I pay attention to every detail

Sometimes it's bad

But even if it means I can make you

Slightly more happy or comfortable

Then I'm satisfied

Can't Sleep

It has gotten to the point

Where I cannot picture doing anything

Without you

Just the mere thought

Sends shivers down my spine

And straight into my soul

How affected am I by this

You might ask

Let me give you an example

I awoke from a nightmare last night

In tears and clutching my pillow

It must have been one of the worst

I have ever experienced

Yet to anyone else

It would not have been so bad

What was it?

Put as simply as possible

I awoke without finding you by my side

Hell

Imagine

Being told that whatever you feel

Is wrong

And that the thoughts

That constantly run through your head

Aren't normal

And medication is the only thing that can

Keep you sane

I wouldn't wish this on anyone

Yet, I am the one who must go through it

I reason with myself

And say that it is deserving due to

All of my past mistakes

And horrible acts I have committed

It makes sense

That I must deal with this

Savior

Life is hard

It's obvious that it would come with

Great disasters and tragedies

For most of my life

I've believed that it had no purpose

And I was never anything more than

A boy who's problems only mattered to him

And the pain that I felt was mine alone

And the fears in my head were unreasonable

So when you came to my life

And told me that you were also hurt

I didn't think much

Until you finally opened my eyes

You said something that made me

Want to change

To get better

To not accept the hardships

And instead fight and fight on

You gave me a purpose

Just by uttering the words

"You make life worth living"

Realization

I remember when your friends told me

That the reason you treated me how you did

Was because I was the first to show genuine

Love towards you

Of course, that didn't make any sense to me

How could someone who "loved" me

Treat me like any other person

Most of the time even worse

You treated me as if I were those who had

Done you wrong

Well now I know exactly what I did wrong

My mistakes were believing that you

Were the one

And believing that it was normal to be

Treated the way I was

Then she came along

And without knowing a thing about me

She already treated me better

Than you could ever have

Till The Next Day, Old Friend

At the end of the day

We get the chance to lay down

And look back at it all

At everyone who is here

Everyone who isn't

And everyone who was

We laugh at our happiest moments

And share a tear for the saddest

We sing for the dreams that remain

And shudder at the thought of "what if"

But it is the end of the day

And sleep is necessary

Time is valuable

And it is best spent enjoying the good

And fighting through the bad

Thank you to those who have stayed

And those who have gone away

Both are invaluable

Both are precious

Both are what make me

Fire

There was recently a fire

Around the corner from the house that I

Grew up in

Everything was lost

There was nothing the family could do

They were only left with what they had with them

I am going through a fire right now

Everything that I've had since I was young

Is now burning up in flames

With my memories being turned into ashes

I have lost my family

I have lost my best friends

All I have is her

Because I take her everywhere I go

I refuse to lose her

For she is what I treasure most

If I were in the fire

She would be the mask that saves me

I am as alone as I have ever been

But even like this

I am not alone

Just a Normal Day

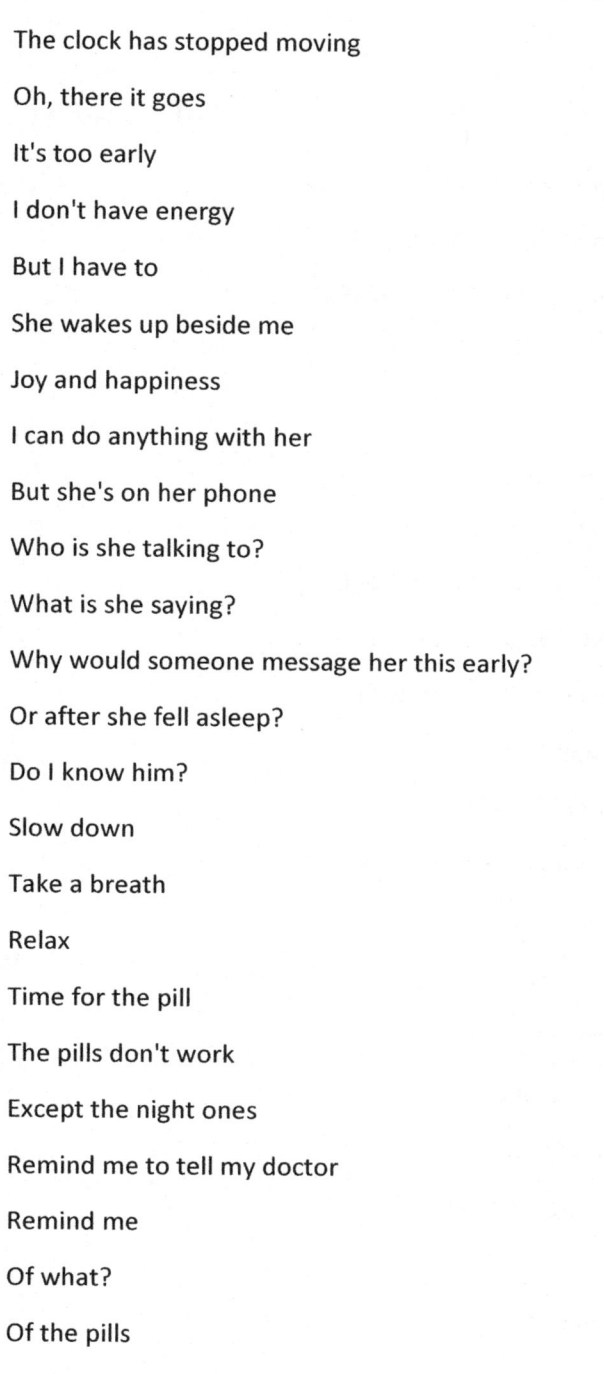

The clock has stopped moving

Oh, there it goes

It's too early

I don't have energy

But I have to

She wakes up beside me

Joy and happiness

I can do anything with her

But she's on her phone

Who is she talking to?

What is she saying?

Why would someone message her this early?

Or after she fell asleep?

Do I know him?

Slow down

Take a breath

Relax

Time for the pill

The pills don't work

Except the night ones

Remind me to tell my doctor

Remind me

Of what?

Of the pills

Ok

Don't forget

Please don't forget.....

Left Standing

But when the dust settles

Who is the one left standing?

You, who took that knife and held it

To your skin

Who took those pills

And wished for peace

Who tightened that noose

And hoped it would relax the soul

Who climbed as high as you could

In hope of seeing a better future

Who is left standing?

In reality, not everyone is.

The number is much smaller than

One would like

But let me tell you

For every knife let go

Or every pill spit out

Every knot loosened

And every ledge climbed off

You will win

You will be the one

Left standing

Humanity

Humans are responsible for most of the

Greatest tragedies in history

Both to nature

And to themselves

We label ourselves as

Cancer to the Earth

And we can only get worse

I admit, I can see how bad we are

I know what kind of things we do to our own

And if we are capable of doing such atrocities

Then what's there to stop us from doing it

To other things

Many humans have given up on humanity

Yet, for some reason, I cannot

Even with the things done to me

Or the things I have witnessed done to others

Even if I tried

Why is that?

Maybe because I keep

Finding a reason to believe

Whether it be as big as helping

A state in distress

Or as small and simple stranger responding

To another's sneeze with a "Bless you"

These things make me believe in humanity

It makes me believe that deep down

We are good.

You're Beautiful

Because every time I tell her

That she's beautiful

She smiles and looks away

Maybe she doesn't believe it

She would rather look away

Than say it isnt so

Well Love, keep looking away

Because even when you won't

Look at me

I'll be looking at you

Because nothing is as beautiful

As you

Reverse Psychology

And tell me, what ever happened

To the good days?

Why have they left and not returned?

I remember when we were together

All of us, just having lunch at our table

Talking and laughing in the face of fate

Daring it to just TRY to separate us

But Fate is petty

It will prove itself by accepting the challenges

Of the weak

And one by one, we fell

Whether it be caused by inner turmoil

Or the simple, damming act of fading away

Our bond which was made of gold

Is now gone, stolen from our hands

So Fate, let me tell you now

That I know better than to challenge you

I know what happens when I lose

So let me be, let me suffer no more

You have taken all but one, and still

I challenge you

To TRY

To let us stay together

Mending The Last Crack

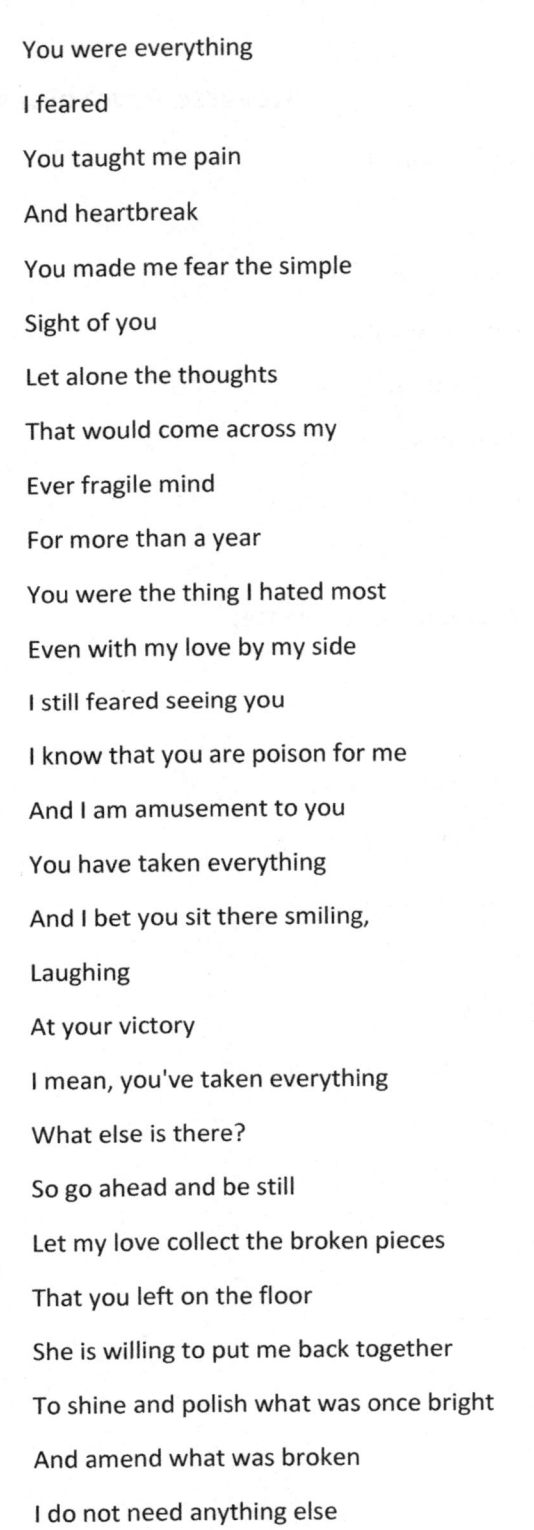

You were everything

I feared

You taught me pain

And heartbreak

You made me fear the simple

Sight of you

Let alone the thoughts

That would come across my

Ever fragile mind

For more than a year

You were the thing I hated most

Even with my love by my side

I still feared seeing you

I know that you are poison for me

And I am amusement to you

You have taken everything

And I bet you sit there smiling,

Laughing

At your victory

I mean, you've taken everything

What else is there?

So go ahead and be still

Let my love collect the broken pieces

That you left on the floor

She is willing to put me back together

To shine and polish what was once bright

And amend what was broken

I do not need anything else

And now that I am at my bottom

Once again

I will climb up

And this time,

I will not do it alone

For she is by my side

And when that ring finally arrives

There will be nothing you can do

I will not fear you

I will not hide from you

In fact, I hope you find what you so desired

Because let me tell you

From personal experience

It is the most amazing feeling in the world

She

Is the most amazing feeling in the world

Father

You were in the army

For most of my life

I remember the feeling

Right before you were sent off

The horrible feeling in knowing

That they were sending you somewhere

Dangerous

And you might not make it back

I remember when you would call

And my mother was happy to hear

Your voice

Even though you and her

Were divorced

Because it meant you were ok

And her child still had a Daddy

I remember the feeling when

You would come back

The smell of your cologne

The scent of your truck

Even the chapstick you would use

I still remember it

I remember how happy I was

When you and Mom decided

To try again

And got married shortly after

I thought this was it

And I was finally going to be

In a normal family

But I also remember the feeling

When I learned that once again

You had cheated on Mom

And the sadness in my heart

In seeing my Mother cry and not stop

And the dread in having lost

The respect for the man

I respected the most

I remember the disappointment

Of finally graduating High School

And still not seeing you there

Because you didn't seem to care

About the great achievement

That your only son accomplished

I remember the feeling

When I heard you through the phone

And how everything I had once

Loved and admired

Was now gone

And instead

Replaced by hatred and despair

I love you Dad

But not as much

As I did before

Scars We Hide

It's funny how scars

Never fade away

As if our body purposely

Keeps them there

To remind us of how we got them

At least half of the scars on my arm

Are from my own doing

If I think really hard

I can remember each

And every one

But those scars do not hurt

No

The scars that hurt

Are the ones we cannot see

With our mortal eyes

The scars we hide with

All of our might inside

Our broken and beaten hearts

These scars always damage

And come back when we are

At our strongest

With the sole purpose

Of bringing you down

These scars are the dangerous ones

They can bring a king to his knees

They can poison you for years

In Fear

How fragile our minds are

And by "our" I mean mine

I look for you among the crowds

If someone has your hair

I look

If someone has your laugh

Or face

Or smile

Or height

Or clothes

I look

But I do not want to see you

I look for you

To stay away

For finding you

Would be bad for me

I am not ready

I probably will never be

But the same can be said

About you

Seeing each other cannot

Be beneficial for anyone

How horrible to constantly

Be living in fear

We Humans

We humans are the only species

That self-harm

There may be those who take it

To the literal sense

And willingly scar their bodies

In the hopes of gaining

Some sort of pleasure or satisfaction

I can understand how

They feel

After all,

Only humans would

Willingly pray for something

That they know

Would cause their downfall

If you think about it

The two are the same

In more ways than one

Silly Boy

How stupid of me

To share with you

Everything that I love

Do not listen to our song

Do not eat at our restaurants

Do not go to our favorite places

Do not wear my favorite shirt

Do not put on that necklace

Do not involve yourself in

Anything that related to us

It wouldn't be fair for you to do it

When I can't

Anyone Else

They ask me what I

Saw in you

My answer was always different

I just couldn't pick only one thing

The way you treated me

Was unjust and unfair

Yet I continued and

Withstood everything

You threw at me

Maybe I liked that

Maybe that's what

Kept me going

The idea to keep fighting

Not giving up

Not letting you win

So call me a masochist

For seeking out that pain

You knew how it would end

But it's as if you are fate

And allowed me to see the error

In my ways

So thank you for this pain

I wish it would not have been you

But frankly my dear

If it were anyone else

It would not have hurt and scarred

First.

The first ones are always

The worst

Even if they are an amazing experience

We constantly go back and compare to it

For our first night out

Sets the mood for all of the others

That are yet to come

Our first love shows us how

Little we were actually prepared

Our firsts are destined

To fail

For if it wouldn't fail

It would not be called first

It would be our only

As if fate knows this

It gives us the fullest

Range of emotions

We could ever feel

And forces us to throw it all

On the table

It is a suicide mission

The idea of giving your all

For something most likely

To fail

How can humans do that so willingly?

So blindly?

So stupidly?

So regretfully?

Inspirational

Inspiration is not fast

It does not come whenever

You call upon it

I, for example

Believed that I actually ran out of

Inspiration

Not because there is nothing inspirational

But because there is nothing different

Before, I wrote of tragedy and of heartbreak

Then, of confusion and indecision

Now, of love and romance

But what comes after that?

Everything has been the same

Since you've arrived

You have singlehandedly

Altered my life

And with great surprise

Forced me into a state of normality

Where I am not always sad

But instead

Always happy

So happy in fact,

That you've made a poet

Run out of words

To describe you

I've Seen Much

I've seen many things this year

I've seen my mother cry

After being cheated on by my father

I've seen her cry the exact tears

When she gave him a second chance

And he did it again

I've seen his new wife

And the new family he has

All while trying to kick us out

Of the house he invited us into

I've seen the most evil person I know

Turn my best friend against me

Something I did not think was possible

I've seen everyone in my family

Turn their backs against me

I've seen new scars on my arm

Along with the old ones that will

Never go away

I've seen so much this year

That it would seem insane to say

That I look forward to the rest of

My life

Because the best thing to ever happen

To me

Was meet you

And with you in my life

I can take another decent year or two

False Hope

Most patients who are Bipolar

Eventually stop taking their medication

Not because their doctor tells them

But because they either don't like

The side effects

Or they believe they are better

I can relate to the side effects reason

But that's not why I stopped taking mine

No, I stopped taking mine

Because I believed that I was stronger

That this illness had nothing on me

And the medications had made me stronger

I felt like I could take on the world

With one hand tied behind my back

Unfortunately, this feeling that I had

Was just a side effect of the illness

The exact opposite of what I was thinking

It's very common, I read

To feel stronger

Than what you actually are

Control

My symptoms

Are under control

After months of switching

And not taking medication

It seems that those horrible thoughts

Are finally kept at bay

My mind can now focus on the more

Important things

Like work

Or taking care of myself

Or what color your eyes turn

When the sun hits them directly

Or how long it will take for

Your natural hair to come out

All of these details about you

That seemed lost

Are now surfacing

And pushing through the dark and evil

Like a match in a dark room

How long will this last?

It does not matter

It is lasting now

And I will enjoy every second of it

Poison in My Mind

Do not leave me alone with my thoughts

They are violent and deadly

They cut more than any knife or blade

And burns more than the strongest fire

They start in my head

And go slowly throughout my body

Like a poison

I've had people say that I am strong

For going through what I've gone through

But I do not believe them

For my thoughts are stronger than I am

And as much as I try to reason with them

They will always come out on top

I have disappointed many people throughout

My life

But remember

I was the first in that line

Freedom

Is this what it feels like?

To be completely sane?

To not have those toxic thoughts

Running around in my brain?

Is this what it is like

When a prisoner is released

After months of torture?

To have the only thought

"I survived"

Whenever he thinks?

Is this what it is like

To be free from my own mind?

Good

I can get used to this

Smile

I remember once

When I was meeting up with

An old high school friend

I was wearing a tee shirt

And her a blouse

And we hugged

When we let go of each other

She looked at my arm

"Oh my God, when did that happen?"

She asked

I just looked at her and smiled

I didn't answer her back

Because it doesn't matter when

Or why

Or how

So I just smiled

And my smile

Was all she needed to know

Holding Hands

We've been dating for months

And yet

I don't know why you do that

What do you mean?

Since we've started dating

You've always held my hand really tight

As if I would blow away

With the slightest wind

Why?

I've always been told that if I love something

To never let it go

Yet many things that I've loved

Have all slipped away

But this time

I refuse to let you go

Made in the USA
Coppell, TX
13 January 2025

44315946R00049